Das Land vor den Bergen
Das bayerische Alpenvorland zwischen Berchtesgaden und Bodensee

The Country below the Mountains
The Bavarian Alpine foreland between Berchtesgaden and Lake Constance

Bernd Römmelt · Michael Lechner

Das Land vor den Bergen

Das bayerische Alpenvorland zwischen Berchtesgaden und Bodensee

The Country below the Mountains
The Bavarian Alpine foreland between Berchtesgaden and Lake Constance

Gewidmet von
Tassilo Glöckler
Wessobrunn / Oberbayern

Austauschschüler 2005

BUCH & KUNSTVERLAG OBERPFALZ

Bibliographische Information Der Deutschen Bibliothek
Die Deutsche Bibliothek verzeichnet diese Publikation in der Deutschen
Nationalbibliografie; detaillierte bibliografische Daten sind im Internet über
http://dnb.ddb.de abrufbar.

© 2004 Buch & Kunstverlag Oberpfalz
Mühlgasse 2, 92224 Amberg
Übersetzung: Philip Wade, 92224 Amberg
Buchgestaltung: Günter Moser, 92260 Ammerthal
Lithographie: Echtzeit Medien, 90429 Nürnberg
Druck: Druckhaus Oberpfalz, 92224 Amberg

ISBN: 3-935719-27-2

Titel: Das Unwetter ist abgezogen, für einen Augenblick kommt noch einmal die Sonne durch am Illasbergsee bei Roßhaupten.
         The storm has passed over, and for a moment the sun comes out again on Lake Illasberg by Roßhaupten.
S. 1:   Vom Schönberg, oberhalb der Ammer gelegen, bietet sich ein herrlicher Blick über das Murnauer Moos auf das Ammergebirge.
         From Schönberg, situated above the River Ammer, you have a splendid view across Murnau Moor to the Ammer mountains.
S. 2:   Der wuchtige Gebirgsstock des Watzmannmassivs beherrscht das Berchtesgadener Land. Links das „Steinerne Meer" mit der
         Schönfeldspitze.
         The huge and mighty Watzmann massif dominates the countryside around Berchtesgaden. To the left, the "Stony Lake" with the
         peak of Schönfeld.
S. 5:   Spätherbst und früher Winter begegnen sich: Blick auf die östliche Karwendelspitze.
         Late autumn and early winter encounter one another: a view of the eastern Karwendel peak.

Es begann alles an einem eiskalten Dezembermorgen im Kochelmoos. Rauhreifbedeckt waren die Bäume. Die beiden Fotografen Bernd Römmelt und Michael Lechner standen an der Loisach und warteten bis die ersten Sonnenstrahlen die Gipfel von Heimgarten und Herzogstand erreichten. Langsam stieg die Sonne über die Berge, tauchte die Landschaft in frühes warmes Licht. Ein Glitzern auf Gräsern und Schilf, von den Wassertümpeln stiegen Nebelschwaden auf, Lichtstreifen vor schattigblauem Hintergrund: das frühe Aufstehen hatte sich gelohnt.

Eingefangen von diesem magischen Morgen im Moos beschlossen sie noch an diesem Tag ein neues, gemeinsames Fotoprojekt, das gesamte bayerische Alpenvorland zwischen Berchtesgaden und dem Bodensee. Jahrelang waren sie um die halbe Welt gereist, hatten für ein Buch über Alaska fotografiert, waren in Kanada und Australien, in Lappland und Slowenien gewesen. Die beiden Münchener hatten fast vergessen, daß einer der schönsten Landstriche Europas direkt vor ihrer Haustüre liegt. Über zwei Jahre haben sie für dieses Buch fotografiert, zu allen Jahreszeiten und beschenkt mit außergewöhnlichen Lichtstimmungen. Die letzten Sonnenstrahlen zum Beispiel, die nach einem Gewitter durch eine Wolkenlücke das Schilf am Illasbergsee im Allgäu golden aufleuchten lassen oder herbstliche Bäume vor kühlblauen Bergflanken. Augenblicke sind zu Lichtblicken geworden.

Die Fotografen waren sich einig, daß nicht nur touristische Sehenswürdigkeiten die Schwerpunkte sein sollten. Natürlich fehlen nicht der Watzmann und die Zugspitze, nicht die Schlösser Herrenchiemsee und Neuschwanstein, nicht der Starnberger See und der Bodensee. Bernd Römmelt und Michael Lechner haben Bekanntes neu gesehen und Unbekanntes dazu entdeckt. So etwas kann man nur schaffen, wenn man dieses bayerische Alpenvorland ganz einfach liebt.

Wichtig war den Fotografen aber auch, und das resultierte aus vielen Begegnungen, den besonderen Menschenschlag im „Land vor den Bergen" zu porträtieren. Der Hirte mit seiner Kuh beim Almabtrieb, die Fischer auf dem Chiemsee, die Frauen mit ihrer Festtracht beim Leonhardiritt in Bad Tölz, die Blaskapelle bei der Fronleichnamsprozession, Geigenbauer und Herrgottsschnitzer – das Land und seine Menschen gehören einfach zusammen.

Dieser Bildband ist Einladung und Aufforderung zugleich, sich im „Land vor den Bergen" umzusehen. Spuren haben die beiden Fotografen genügend gelegt.

It all began one icy cold December morning on Kochel Moor. The trees were covered with hoar frost, and the two photographers Bernd Römmelt and Michael Lechner were standing by the River Loisach, waiting for the first rays of sunlight to reach the peaks of Heimgarten and Herzogstand. Slowly, the sun rose over the mountains, steeping the landscape in a warm, early morning light. The grass and reeds glittered, clouds of mist arose from the ponds, and streaks of light contrasted with the shady blue background. Getting up early had been worth it after all.

Entranced by this magic morning on the moor, they decided that very day to venture out on a new photographic project together: the whole of the Bavarian Alpine foreland between Berchtesgaden and Lake Constance. For years they'd been travelling round the world, they'd taken photographs for a book about Alaska, they'd been to Canada and Australia, to Lapland and Slovenia.

Originally from Munich, they'd almost forgotten, however, that one of the most beautiful stretches of landscape in Europe is here, right on their doorstep. They spent over two years on the photographs for this book, in all seasons, to be rewarded with extraordinary moods, captured by the light. The last rays of sunlight, for instance, which, peeping through a break in the clouds after a storm, lend the reeds on Lake Illasberg in Allgäu a golden hue, or autumnal trees contrasting with the cool blue mountainside. Moments in time transformed into moments in light.

The photographers were in agreement that the focal point of their work was not only to be the typical tourist sights. Of course, Watzmann and Zugspitze have been included, as have the castles of Herrenchiemsee and Neuschwanstein, Lake Starnberg and Lake Constance. Bernd Römmelt and Michael Lechner have looked at the well-known from a new viewpoint, thereby discovering the unknown. And yet, it's only possible to create something like this if you are truly in love with this part of Bavaria, the Alpine foothills.

It was also important for the photographers, though, to portray the especial type of people in this "country below the mountains", something that resulted from numerous meetings with the people themselves. The farmer driving his cattle down from the Alpine pastures, the fishermen on Lake Chiem, the women with their festive dress at the Parade of St. Leonhard in Bad Tölz, the brass band at the Corpus Christi procession, violin makers and carvers of crucifixes and other religious figures – the countryside and its people simply belong together.

This collection of photographs is at one and the same time an invitation and a request to pay a visit to the "country below the mountains": the two photographers have left sufficient clues behind to guide you.

Schon im Jahre 1898 schrieb der bekannte Reiseschrift-steller Heinrich Noe – und der kannte sich aus in den Bergen –: „Das Berchtesgadener Land ist der Yellow-stonepark der deutschen Alpen, die großartigsten Schau-stücke derselben liegen nirgends so vor deiner Tür wie hier", und Ludwig Ganghofer schreibt man den Satz zu: „Herr, wen du liebhast, den lässest du fallen in dieses Land!" Alles nur Schwärmereien? Sicher nicht! Dieser südöstlichste Zipfel Bayerns ist wahrlich eine Bilder-buchlandschaft. Sie wird überragt vom 2713 m hohen Watzmann, dessen über 1800 m hohe Ostwand 1881 erstmals von Johann Grill, Kederbacher genannt, durch-stiegen wurde und die auch heute noch viele Bergsteiger in ihren Bann zieht.

1978 hat man den Nationalpark Berchtesgaden einge-richtet, der Naturschutz und Tourismus versöhnt, der zeigt, daß die beiden doch unter einen Hut zu bringen sind, wenn guter Wille von beiden Seiten vorhanden ist. Stiftskirche und Kloster, Eispaläste und Höhlen, einsame Steige und aussichtsreiche Almen und natürlich der Königssee als Juwel des Ganzen ziehen alljährlich viele Tausende in diese Region. Je nach Sonneneinstrahlung wechselt der See seine Farben, mal tiefgrün, mal dun-kelblau, und wenn dann noch der Bootsmann auf seiner Trompete bläst und das Echo von den Felswänden zurückkommt, sitzt man andächtig im Boot und denkt an die Sätze von Ganghofer und Noe.

As early as 1898, the well-known travel writer Heinrich Noe – and he knew the mountains like the back of his own hand – put it thus: "The countryside around Berch-tesgaden is the Yellowstone Park of the German Alps, of which there are nowhere else such fabulous showpieces as here, on your very doorstep," and it is to Ludwig Ganghofer that the following sentence is ascribed: "Lord, whomsoever thou lovest, so let him fall into this country-side!" Nothing but gushing enthusiasm? Most certainly not. This south-easternmost tip of Bavaria is without doubt a picture book landscape. It is dominated by the Watzmann, 8,901 ft high, of which the eastern wall, over 5,900 ft high, was first climbed by Johann Grill, nick-named "Kederbacher", and which even today still holds many a mountain climber spellbound.

In 1978 the Berchtesgaden National Park was inaugurated, reconciling conservation and tourism, and illustrating how the two can indeed exist together, provided that the will on both sides is there.

The collegiate church and monastery, indoor palaces of ice and caves, lonely mountain paths and pastures with picturesque views, and of course King's Lake, the crowning glory, attract many thousands to the region year by year. Depending on how the sunlight falls, the lake changes its colours: sometimes it's dark green, sometimes dark blue; if then the boatswain blows his trumpet and the echo returns from the rock face, you sit absorbed in the boat, and the words of Ganghofer and Noe seem to ring true.

Das Berchtesgadener Land
Im Reich des Königs Watzmann

The Countryside around Berchtesgaden – In the realm of King Watzmann

Langsam kämpft sich die aufgehende Sonne durch den Morgennebel – ein traumhafter Sommertag am Untersberg beginnt.
Slowly, the rising sun fights its way through the morning mist – a dreamlike summer's day starting at Untersberg.

9

Blütenpracht auf den Blumenwiesen im Nationalpark Berchtes-gaden: Enzian, Hahnenfuß, Margerite, Alpenprimel und Kuckucks-lichtnelke in verschwenderischer Fülle.

A magnificent array of blossoms adorn the meadows in Berchtesgaden National Park: an extravagant abundance of gentian, buttercups, daisies, Alpine primroses and cuckooflowers.

10

Da rastet man gerne, da macht man gerne Brotzeit, auf der Gotzenalm mit der zerklüfteten Watzmannostwand dahinter.

Gotzen meadow, a place to rest for a while and enjoy a typical Bavarian picnic, with the rugged east wall of Watzmann in the background.

Die Bäuerinnen sind stolz auf ihre geraniengeschmückten Fenster und Balkone.

The farmers' wives are proud of their windows and balconies decorated with geraniums.

*Einfach einladend, die alten bemalten Holzhäuser in Königssee
strahlen Würde und Standhaftigkeit zugleich aus.*

*Simply inviting, the old, painted wooden houses in Königssee evince
both dignity and fortitude.*

Der Almabtrieb von der Fischunkenalm mit Booten über den Königssee ist einer der bekanntesten in ganz Oberbayern. Sicher war es ein gutes Almjahr gewesen.

The tradition of driving cattle down from Fischunken pasture by boat across King's Lake is one of the most famous throughout Upper Bavaria. It was most certainly a good year up on the pastures.

Mit kalten Nächten kündigt sich der Herbst an. Morgennebel überziehen den Hintersee, die aufgehende Sonne vergoldet das Wasser.

As the nights get colder, autumn announces its arrival. Morning mists close in on Lake Hinter, and the rising sun turns the water golden.

St. Bartholomä ist am besten mit dem Schiff zu erreichen.
Links dahinter ragt die Watzmannostwand auf.
Schon viele Bergsteigertragödien haben sich in ihr abgespielt.

St. Bartholomew's is best reached by ship.
Behind it, on the left, the soaring east wall of Watzmann, where
many a mountain climbing tragedy has taken place.

Die Kneifelspitze ist einer der schönsten Aussichtsberge im Berchtesgadener Land. Weit schweift der Blick über Berchtesgaden auf Watzmann und Hochkalter.

Kneifel peak is one of the most beautiful mountains for surveying the area around Berchtesgaden. You have a fine panorama over Berchtesgaden itself to Watzmann and Hochkalter.

18

Sagenumwoben ist der Untersberg. Kaiser Friedrich Barbarossa soll hier mit seinen Getreuen schlafen und die Zwerge „Untersbergmandl" nach Gold und Edelsteinen schürfen.

Steeped in legend, Untersberg is where Emperor Frederick Barbarossa, together with his faithful followers, is said to sleep, and the Untersberg Dwarves reputedly dig for gold and precious stones.

*Bekannt aus vielen deutschen Berg- und Heimatfilmen,
das Kircherl in der Ramsau mit der Reiteralpe im Hintergrund.*

*Well-known from a number of patriotic German films
about the mountains, the small church in Ramsau,
with Reiter Alp in the background.*

Eine uralte Kulturlandschaft ist dieses Land zwischen dem Inn im Westen und der Traun und unteren Alz im Osten, den Bergen im Süden und einer gedachten Linie in der Höhe Wasserburgs im Norden. Die Römer hatten über vier Jahrhunderte dies Land im Besitz, sie haben ihre Spuren hinterlassen. Schon im 8. Jahrhundert wurden hier die ersten Klöster gegründet. Der bayerische Geschichtsschreiber Aventinus merkt dazu an: „...ains den frauen das andere den mannen". Auch heute noch ist das Kloster auf der Fraueninsel eines der beliebtesten Ausflugsziele. Unter schattigen Bäumen sitzen, eine Chiemseerenke auf dem Teller und die prächtige Kulisse von Hochries, Hochgern und Kampenwand vor sich, Segelboote auf glitzerndem Wasser, da spricht man gerne von erfüllten Tagen.

Natürlich darf man, spricht man über dieses Land, das Königsschloß von Ludwig II. auf der Herreninsel nicht vergessen. Nach dem Vorbild von Versailles hat er es erbauen lassen. Innen wurde es nie fertig- wahrscheinlich ist dem König das Geld ausgegangen-, aber Schloß und Park, Springbrunnen und Pferdekutschen versetzen die Besucher in eine andere, weit zurückliegende Zeit.

Über 80 Quadratkilometer ist der Chiemsee groß, und doch ist das nur ein Bruchteil jener Ausdehnung, die er kurz nach der letzten Eiszeit hatte. Die stillen kleinen Seen, wie Simssee und Perlhamer See, Langbürgner und Seeoner See, sind die Reste jenes großen einstigen Gewässers.

This stretch of countryside between the River Inn to the west, the Rivers Traun and Lower Alz to the east, the mountains to the south and an imaginary line running through Wasserburg to the north has an age-old cultural history. For over four centuries, this part of Bavaria was occupied by the Romans, and they certainly left their traces behind. It was here that, as early as the 8th century, the first monasteries were founded. The Bavarian chronicler Aventinus noted: "… one for the womenfolk, the other for the menfolk." Still today, the monastery on Fraueninsel is one of the most popular destinations for a day trip. Sitting in the shade of the trees, a Chiemsee fish on your plate, the splendid scenery of Hochries, Hochgern and Kampenwand in front of you, and sailing boats on the glistening water: it's days like this you never want to end!

Of course, when talking about this landscape, we should not forget the king's castle of Ludwig II on Herreninsel, which he had built on the example of Versailles. Within, it was never finished, probably because the king ran out of money, but the castle and gardens, fountains and horse carriages take visitors back to a very different time, long, long ago.

Lake Chiem is over 30 square miles in size, and yet that is only a fraction of the distance over which it extended shortly after the last Ice Age. The calm little lakes, such as Lake Sims and Perlhamer, Langbürgner and Seeoner Lakes, are the remnants of what was once one large inland sea.

Der Chiemgau

Bayerisches Meer und Insel-Märchenschloß

Chiemgau – Bavarian lakes and a fairy tale castle on an island

*Bei dieser Morgenstimmung, diesem Leuchten über noch nachtschwarzen Bergflanken,
ist die kalte Nacht im Schlafsack auf der Kampenwand schnell vergessen.*

*In such a mood, early in the morning, as day breaks over mountainsides still pitch-black,
you quickly forget the cold night you spent in your sleeping bag on Kampenwand.*

Noch im Morgengrauen fahren die Chiemseefischer
hinaus auf den See. Ob sich der Fang auf Renken, Forellen, Hechte
und Zander lohnen wird?

The day has not yet broken, and fishermen on Lake Chiem
take their boats out. Who knows whether it'll be worth trying to
catch, trout, pike and zander?

Auf dem Samerberg holt der Bauer Grünfutter für seine Kühe. *On Samerberg the farmer gathers green fodder for his cows.*

Die Kirche St. Lambert der ehemaligen Benediktinerabtei von Seeon spiegelt sich im kleinen See. Einst eilte der elfjährige Mozart durch die Gänge und musizierte mit dem Pater auf der Orgel. Heute befindet sich im Kloster eine bekannte Bildungsstätte.

Blühende Farbenpracht des Spätsommers im Garten der Benediktinerinnen auf der Fraueninsel mit Zinnien, Sonnenhut, Rosen und vielen Kräutern.

A splendid array of colourful blossoms in late summer in the Benedictine sisters' garden on Fraueninsel, with zinnias, coneflowers, roses and a wide variety of herbs.

St. Lambert's church, formerly part of the Benedictine abbey of Seeon, reflected in the little lake. This was where, at the age of 11, Mozart once hurried along the corridors and played music with one of the fathers on the organ. Today, the monastery houses a well-known educational establishment.

27

Die Ratzinger Höhe am Westufer des Chiemsees gilt als einer
der schönsten Aussichtsplätze auf See, Inseln und Chiemgauer
Alpen. Dieser prächtige Blick lockte schon immer die
Landschaftsmaler an.

Ratzinger Heights on the west bank of Lake Chiem has the
reputation of being one of the finest spots for a view of the lake,
the islands and the Chiemgau Alps. This splendid outlook
has always had a special attraction for landscape painters.

Morgennebel überziehen den Chiemsee
und das angrenzende Moos.

Morning mist covering Lake Chiem
and the adjacent moor.

Es ist noch ruhig am See, Schwanenpaar vor der Kulisse
der Chiemgauer Alpen.

Things are still quiet by the lake: a pair of swans against
the backdrop of the Chiemgau Alps.

So still ist es nur am frühen Morgen, bevor die Dampfer die
Tagesgäste zur Herreninsel bringen. Denn dieses Märchenschloß
von König Ludwig II. gehört in jedes Besuchsprogramm;
es entführt in längst vergangene Zeiten.

It's only early in the morning that everything is so peaceful,
before the steamers bring the daytrippers to Herreninsel.
Because the fairy tale castle of King Ludwig II is on every itinerary,
visitors are whisked away to times of yesteryear.

Gar nicht weit entfernt vom Trubel am Chiemsee findet man an den Wassern der Eggstätter Seenplatte ein Paradies der Ruhe und Abgeschiedenheit.

Not so very far removed from the hustle and bustle on Lake Chiem, a paradise of peace and solitude by the waters of Eggstätter lake district.

Nach einer kühlen Nacht dampft das Wasser nach Sonnenaufgang, ein kostenloses Schauspiel der Natur für alle Frühaufsteher.

After a cold night the water starts to vaporize after sunrise, a play put on by nature for the benefit of early risers, all free of charge.

Die stimmungsvollsten Bilder entstehen oft in den ersten Stunden des anbrechenden Tages. In der Nähe von Rimsting geht der Blick über das unbewegte Wasser des Sees auf die Gipfel von Hochgern, Hochplatte und Kampenwand (v. l. n. r.). Im Taleinschnitt der Tiroler Ache ist noch schemenhaft das Massiv der Loferer Steinberge zu erkennen.

The most evocative photographs can often be taken in the first few hours as a new day breaks. Near Rimsting you have a fine view over the calm water of the lake to the summits of Hochgern, Hochplatte and Kampenwand (from left to right). In the valley section of the River Tyroler Ache, the outline of the massive Lofer Stone Mountains can still be discerned.

Schon den geistlichen Herren der Benediktiner gefiel es am Tegernsee so gut, daß sie hier eines der ältesten Klöster Bayerns gründeten, und König Max I. Joseph hat diese Klosteranlage zu seinem Sommersitz gemacht. Heute sind es mehr die Wanderer, die in dieser Bilderbuchlandschaft auf die Berge steigen. Sie wachsen hier nicht schroff in den Himmel, sind eher sanft gewölbt, manche mit Felskronen geziert, wie Plankenstein, Roßstein oder Ruchenköpfe. Und wer einmal etwas nostalgisch auf den Berg kommen will, besteige die Zahnradbahn auf den Wendelstein, die erstmals 1912 auf den Gipfel ratterte. Na ja! Der Gipfel ist schon arg verbaut, aber einen schönen Blick hat man noch immer.
In Bayrischzell ist 1883 der erste bayerische Trachtenverein gegründet worden, der Kiem Pauli hat in Bad Kreuth gelebt und heute noch gibt es hier jene unverfälschte Volksmusik- und Bauerntheaterszene, die sich in die Herzen spielt und musiziert. Und noch einen dürfen wir hier nicht vergessen, den Wildschütz Georg Jennerwein, der 1877 in den Wäldern der Bodenschneid von einem Jäger erschossen wurde. Auf seinem Grab liegen auch heute noch immer frische Blumen und im Lied ist er sowieso unvergessen.

Even the gentlemen of the Benedictine clergy liked Lake Tegern so much that they founded one of the oldest monasteries in Bavaria here, and King Max I Joseph turned the monastery grounds into his summer residence. Today, the hikers tend to be the ones to climb up the mountains in this picture book landscape, mountains that don't rise straight up to the sky but look more like gentle domes, some of them adorned with crowns of rocks, such as Plankenstein, Roßstein or Ruchenköpfe. And if you prefer taking more nostalgic a trip up the mountain, get on the cog railway up Wendelstein, which first rattled to the summit in 1912. It's true, the summit has been rather spoilt by construction work, but you still have a fine view.
It was in Bayrischzell that the first Bavarian traditional costumes society was founded in 1883; Kiem Pauli lived in Bad Kreuth, and even today the traditions of genuine Bavarian folk music and peasants' theatres are kept alive for all to enjoy. And there's something else we mustn't forget: the poacher Georg Jennerwein, who was shot and killed by a hunter in the Bodenschneid Forests in 1877. Even today, fresh flowers are left on his grave, and anyway the song about him still hasn't been forgotten.

Das bayerische Oberland
Gipfelkircherl, Seen und Sommerfrische
The Bavarian Highland – Churches on summits, lakes and summer freshness

Wie von riesigen Scheinwerfern angestrahlt, der Malerwinkel in Rottach-Egern am Tegernsee mit der Pfarrkirche St. Laurentius.
As if lit up by huge floodlights, Painters' Corner in Rottach-Egern on Lake Tegern, with the parish church of St. Laurentius.

Vom Wallberg am Südende des Tegernsees blickt man nach Norden auf den glitzernden See und das Alpenvorland, im Süden erheben sich Sonnwendjoch, Schinder und Risserkogel.

From Wallberg at the southern end of Lake Tegern you can look north to the glittering lake and the Alpine foothills; to the south, the towering mountains of Sonnwendjoch, Schinder and Risserkogel.

Zur Sonnwend am 21. Juni mit der kürzesten Nacht des Jahres werden auf vielen Gipfeln der bayerischen Alpen traditionell die Sonnwendfeuer entzündet – wie hier am Wallberg.

On 21 June, to traditionally celebrate the summer solstice and the shortest night of the year, bonfires are lit on many summits of the Bavarian Alps – as here on Wallberg.

Lange vor Sonnenaufgang leuchtet der feurige Himmel über dem
1838 m hohen Wendelstein. Er ist ein beliebter Aussichtsberg.

Long before sunrise, the red glow of the sky above Wendelstein,
6,029 ft high. This is a popular mountain for spectacular views.

Herbstlich leuchtendes Laub, spitzer Kirchturm,
See und Berge, fertig ist das Idyll wie hier am Schliersee mit
Blick auf Brecherspitze, Jägerkamp und Spitzingsattel.

Leaves in bright, autumnal shades, a pointed church spire,
a lake and mountains – the perfect idyll, as here on Lake Schlier
with a view of Brecherspitze, Jägerkamp and Spitzingsattel.

„Mich wolln s` fotografiern? Ich bin doch schon alt und greislig!"
Mitnichten, ein oberbayerisches Gesicht in Tölz.

"You don't want a photo of me, all old and grey!"
Not at all – a typical Upper Bavarian face in Tölz.

Ein bißchen Skepsis unter Trachtenhut und Gamsbart.
Junges Mädel in Tegernseer Tracht.

Looking a little sceptical beneath her traditional hat with
its tuft of chamois hair, a young girl in her Tegernsee costume.

„Mich wolln s' fotografiern? Ich bin doch schon alt und greislig!"
Mitnichten, ein oberbayerisches Gesicht in Tölz.

"You don't want a photo of me, all old and grey!"
Not at all – a typical Upper Bavarian face in Tölz.

Ein bißchen Skepsis unter Trachtenhut und Gamsbart.
Junges Mädel in Tegernseer Tracht.

Looking a little sceptical beneath her traditional hat with
its tuft of chamois hair, a young girl in her Tegernsee costume.

„Mich wolln s` fotografiern? Ich bin doch schon alt und greislig!"
Mitnichten, ein oberbayerisches Gesicht in Tölz.

"You don't want a photo of me, all old and grey!"
Not at all – a typical Upper Bavarian face in Tölz.

Ein bißchen Skepsis unter Trachtenhut und Gamsbart.
Junges Mädel in Tegernseer Tracht.

Looking a little sceptical beneath her traditional hat with
its tuft of chamois hair, a young girl in her Tegernsee costume.

*Direkt neben der Auto-
bahn München–Salz-
burg: Tausende fahren
täglich vorbei an der
dem Heiligen Marinus
geweihten Kapelle bei
Wilparting.
Die mächtige Linde
ragt in den Himmel, die
Berge um den Wendel-
stein tragen noch ihre
Schneehauben.*

*Every day, thousands
drive past the chapel
near Wilparting
dedicated to
St. Marinus, directly
adjacent to the Munich-
Salzburg motorway.
The mighty linden tree
stretches into the sky,
the mountain peaks
around Wendelstein are
still snow-capped.*

44

„Heiliger St. Leonhard, schütz unser Vieh und Pferd."
Beim Ritt und beim Umzug zu Ehren des Heiligen wird in Tölz
die Festtagstracht angelegt.

"Holy St. Leonhard, protect our cattle and horses."
At the parade and procession in honour of the saint, people
in Tölz traditionally put on their festive costumes.

Der Winter ist einge-
kehrt im Luisental bei
Gmund am Tegernsee.

Winter has come to
Luise valley near
Gmund on Lake Tegern.

Im Isarwinkel an der
Grenze zwischen Bayern
und Österreich schützt
das alte Bauernhaus vor
der Kälte des Winters.

In the angular turn that
the River Isar takes on
the border between
Bavaria and Austria,
an old farmhouse
provides protection
against the winter cold.

Mondlicht und erstes
Tageslicht in der Morgen-
dämmerung an einem
frostig kalten Morgen am
Irschenberg.

Moonlight and the first
light of dawn compete
as day breaks on a cold,
frosty morning on
Irschenberg.

46

Stille eines Wintertages, fernab von Liften und
Pistenzauber am Irschenberg.

The peace and quiet of a winter's day, far removed from the lifts
and the attraction of ski runs on Irschenberg.

Nach langem Warten spitzt die Sonne über die Berge.
Vom Gut Kaltenbrunn aus schweift der Blick über den
Tegernsee und die Berge.

After a long wait, the sun peeps out from behind the
mountains. From Kaltenbrunn Estate you have a panoramic
view across Lake Tegern and the mountains.

Die Maler der Künstlergruppe „Der Blaue Reiter" wußten schon, warum sie sich ausgerechnet hier niederließen. Wassily Kandinsky, Gabriele Münter und Franz Marc arbeiteten in dieser Gegend, wo anscheinend der Gleichklang von Natur, Dörfern und Klöstern künstlerische Schaffensprozesse beeinflusste. Die Blicke über das Murnauer Moos hin zur gezackten Horizontlinie der Berge ist immer wieder ein visuelles Erlebnis.

Das Kloster Benediktbeuren, um 750 gegründet, war über lange Zeiten ein Hort der Wissenschaft und der Kunst. Hier wurde die „Carmina Burana" aufgeschrieben, eine Sammlung deutscher und lateinischer Lieder von fahrenden Schülern. Vielleicht waren es die vielen Kirchen und Klöster, die diesem liebenswerten Land zum Namen „Pfaffenwinkel" verhalfen. Das klingt heute fast ein bißchen respektlos, doch in früheren Zeiten wurde die Geistlichkeit von der Bevölkerung so bezeichnet.

Religiöses Brauchtum ist hier noch unverfälscht lebendig. Man denke nur an die Fronleichnamsprozession in Seehausen am Staffelsee, wo auf festlich geschmückten Booten unterm „Himmel" das Allerheiligste über den See gerudert wird. Und wenn sich dann noch über dem „kleinen Himmel" ein großer Bilderbuchhimmel wölbt, ist die bayerische Seele rundum zufrieden.

The painters belonging to the group of artists called "The Blue Rider" certainly knew why, of all places, they should settle here. Wassily Kandinsky, Gabriele Münter and Franz Marc worked in this region, where apparently the harmony of nature, villages and monasteries had an influence on the creative process of the artist. The views across Murnau Moor to the jagged line of mountains on the horizon are a visual experience over and over again.

The monastery of Benediktbeuren, founded about 750, was for long periods a refuge for arts and sciences. This is where "Carmina Burana" was written down, a collection of German and Latin songs by wandering scholars. Perhaps it was the multitude of churches and monasteries that gave this lovely region its nickname of "Pfaffenwinkel" (Parsons Corner). Today, that sounds rather disrespectful, but in earlier times people referred to the clergy in this way.

Here, religious traditions are still genuinely alive: we need only think of the Corpus Christi procession in Seehausen on Lake Staffel, where the Most Holy Sacrament is borne beneath the baldachin, called the "Heaven" in German, on festively decorated rowing boats across the lake. And then, if above this little heaven a huge picture book heaven spreads out like a dome, the Bavarian spirit is at one with the world.

Der Pfaffenwinkel

Klöster, Kirchen und „ Der Blaue Reiter"

Pfaffenwinkel – Monasteries, churches and "The Blue Rider"

„Still ruhet der See, er ladet zum Bade...". Denkt man nicht unwillkürlich an das Lied des Fischerjungen aus „Wilhelm Tell" von Friedrich von Schiller bei diesem Bild vom Kochelsee.

"Calm rests o'er the lake, to bathe in its waters ..." Do we not think instinctively of the fisher-boy's song from "William Tell" by Friedrich von Schiller when we see this photograph of Lake Kochel?

Das Murnauer Moos ist ein Landschaftsschutzgebiet mit seltener Flora und Fauna. Kuckuckslichtnelke, Trollblume, Sibirische Schwertlilie und Bachnelkenwurz stehen stellvertretend für den Artenreichtum.

Murnau Moor is a conservation area with rare flora and fauna. Cuckooflowers, globeflowers, irises and avens are only a few examples of such rich diversity.

Wie ein Aquarell mutet dieses Bild mit seinen zarten Farben an. Über dem Sattel rechts vom Jochberg sieht man die Karwendelgruppe.

With its pastel shades, this photograph gives the impression of being a water-colour painting. Above the col to the right of Jochberg we can see the Karwendel Range.

Nebel steigt aus dem feuchten Murnauer Moos auf. Im Hintergrund
färbt die Morgensonne das Zugspitzmassiv.

Mist rising from damp Murnau Moor. In the background,
the morning sun lends colour to the Zugspitze massif.

Der Staffelsee bei Murnau mit seinen sieben Inseln ist ein beliebter Badesee. In dieser Jahreszeit ist es noch ruhig an seinen Ufern.

Lake Staffel, near Murnau, with its seven isles is a very popular lake for bathing. At this time of year the banks are still peaceful.

Boarische Madln und Wadln.

Bavarian girls in their traditional dresses ... and a fine pair of knees!

56

Frömmigkeit und Brauchtum unter weißblauem Himmel bei
der Fronleichnamsprozession in Seehausen am Staffelsee.
Trachtenkapelle und Honoratioren, Fahnenabordnungen
der Vereine und der „Himmel" haben gerade noch
Platz auf dem Schiff.

Beneath a true Bavarian blue and white sky, religion and
tradition hand in hand at the Corpus Christi procession in
Seehausen on Lake Staffel. A brass band in traditional costume,
town celebrities, flag-bearers from local clubs and the
baldachin just have room on the ship.

An den kleinen und sauberen Bergbächen findet man noch die
Wasseramsel, die taucht, schwimmt und unter Wasser Insekten und
kleine Schnecken als Nahrung sucht.

In the clean, little mountain streams the water ouzel can
still be found, diving, swimming and searching under water for
insects and small snails to eat.

Die Schleierfälle bei Kreut in der Ammerschlucht
mit ihren faszinierenden Wasserspielen.

Schleier Falls near Kreut in the Gorge of Ammer,
with its fascinating waterworks.

*Die Satellitenschüsseln bei Raisting südlich von Dießen
bilden inmitten von Wiesen und Feldern einen außergewöhnlichen
Kontrast in der Landschaft.*

*Satellite dishes in the middle of meadows and
fields near Raisting, south of Dießen, form an unusual
contrast to the landscape.*

Das bayerische „Urkloster" Benediktbeuren an einem kalten Herbstmorgen. Im Hintergrund der markante Gipfel des Herzogstands.

Benediktbeuren, the most typical of all Bavarian monasteries, on a cold autumn morning. In the background, the prominent summit of Herzogstand.

Vom Leibersberg aus sieht man über den Riegsee bei Murnau auf den markanten Dreiecksgipfel der Alpspitze, links im Bild. Von hier zieht sich der Jubiläumsgrat bis zur Zugspitze.

Looking out from Leibersberg, you have a view across Lake Rieg near Murnau to the striking triangular summit of Alpspitze, on the left. From here, the Jubiläumsgrat ridge extends to the Zugspitze.

Die ersten Sonnenstrahlen lassen die Grate der Berge aufleuchten. Der Kochelsee am Loisachabfluß dampft an einem eisigen Januarmorgen, Rauhreif hat Bäume und Sträucher überzuckert.

The first rays of sunlight illuminate the crests of the mountains. On an icy January morning, water vapour rises from Lake Kochel, from which the River Loisach flows, and hoar frost has coated trees and shrubs with what looks like icing.

Graziös stehen die
Birken vor blauem
Himmel, winterliche
Traumlandschaft
im Kochelmoos nahe
Unterau. Lautlos
schwebt der Ballon über
Fluren und Dörfer,
nur ab und zu unter-
brochen vom Surren
des Brenners.

Birch trees stand grace-
fully against a blue sky
in this dreamlike winter
landscape on Kochel
Moor, near Unterau.
The balloon hovers
silently over villages and
open farmland, only
interrupted now and
again by the buzzing of
the burner.

Am 27. August 1820 bestiegen der bayerische Leutnant Karl Naus und seine Begleiter zum Zwecke der Landvermessung das erste Mal die Zugspitze. Mit 2962 Metern ist sie der höchste Berg Deutschlands und zu ihren Füßen breitet sich das Werdenfelser Land aus, das seinen Namen von der gleichnamigen Burg am Fuße des Kramer hat. In früheren Zeiten wurde diese Region als „Goldenes Landl" bezeichnet, hatte doch der Fernhandel manchen Orten bescheidenen Wohlstand geschenkt.

Heute ist der Fremdenverkehr die Haupteinnahmequelle – auch mit all seinen Schattenseiten. An schönen Tagen findet man kaum ein ruhiges Plätzchen am Eibsee, das Kloster Ettal ist dann kein Ort der Stille und durch Schloß Linderhof werden Besuchergruppen im Eiltempo geschleust.

Aber es gibt auch Plätze, wo man alleine ist: am Geroldsee und am Barmsee, im Murnauer Moos mit seinem herrlichen Blick auf Wetterstein und Karwendel – alle wollen wir nicht verraten.

Nicht nur berühmte Kirchen laden ein zu Gebet und Kunstbetrachtung, auch in kleinen Kapellen finden sich so manche Schätze. Vielleicht stammen sie sogar von den Holzschnitzern aus Oberammergau, wo alle zehn Jahre das weltbekannte Passionsspiel aufgeführt wird.

Mittenwald ist bekannt für seinen Geigenbau, untrennbar verbunden mit dem Namen Matthias Klotz. Und vor den behäbigen Häusern mit den Lüftlmalereien steht man staunend und bewundernd: traditionelle Freskokunst, scheinbar Zeiten überdauernd.

On 27 August 1820, the Bavarian lieutenant Karl Naus and his companions ascended the Zugspitze for the first time for the purpose of surveying it. With a height of 9,718 ft, it's the highest mountain in Germany, and at its foot the Werdenfelser region spreads out, christened after the castle at the foot of Kramer of the same name. In earlier times this region was characterized as "Golden Country" since trade with far-off lands had resulted in many places becoming modestly wealthy. Today, tourism is the main source of income – with all its drawbacks.

On fine days you can hardly find a quiet place to sit by Lake Eib, Ettal Monastery is then no longer a refuge of peace and calm, and groups of visitors are channelled through Linderhof Castle at high speed.

However, there are also places where you can be alone: by Lake Gerold and Lake Barm, on Murnau Moor with its fabulous view of Wetterstein and Karwendel – we don't want to disclose all of them!

Not only famous churches invite the passer-by to pray and view the works of art; many a treasure can also be found in little chapels. Perhaps they even originate from the wood carvers in Oberammergau, where every ten years the world-famous Passion Play is performed.

Mittenwald is well-known for its violin making industry, inseparably connected to the name of Matthias Klotz. And standing in front of the sedate houses with their historic wall paintings (called "Lüftlmalerei" in German, perhaps because they were executed in the fresh air), you can only stare in wonder and admiration at this traditional fresco art that, it seems, has survived throughout the ages and will continue to do so.

Werdenfelser Land und Ammergau
„Goldenes Landl" im Schatten der Zugspitze
The Werdenfelser region and Ammergau – "Golden Country" in the shade of the Zugspitze

Krokusblüte auf den Wiesen bei Klais, dahinter die verschneiten Gipfel des Karwendels.
Crocuses blossoming on meadows near Klais; in the background the snow-capped peaks of Karwendel.

Noch etwas geknickt von der Kälte
der Nacht sind die Trollblumen
am Geroldsee, einem Kleinod in
imposanter Landschaft.

On Lake Gerold, a gem in the
middle of imposing scenery.
The globeflowers are still hanging
their heads from the cold of the night.

Die Buckelwiesen bei Klais gehören
zu den artenreichsten in ganz Bayern.
Im Frühsommer entfalten sie ihre
ganze Pracht.

The Buckel meadows near Klais have one
of the highest levels of biodiversity in the
whole of Bavaria. In early summer they
display their full splendour.

69

Die „Strahdrischeln" am südlichen Ende des
Murnauer Mooses weisen den Weg ins Werdenfelser Land.

The typical stacks of hay, straw and reeds at the southern end of
Murnau Moor point the way to the Werdenfelser region.

Herbstliche Farben am Ufer des Geroldsees mit den Heuschobern, oft alt, verwittert und windschief geworden durch viele Jahrzehnte.

Autumnal colours on the banks of Lake Gerold with its hay barns, often old, weather-beaten and crooked from decades of exposure to the elements.

Schloß Linderhof im Graswangtal ist ein kleines, dem Rokoko-stil nachempfundenes Schlößchen. Man spricht von der eigenwilligsten Schöpfung Ludwigs II.

Linderhof Castle in the Graswang valley is a little castle in imitation rococo style. It is said to be Ludwig II's most un-conventional creation.

72

Der Monopteros im Park von Schloß Linderhof empfängt die ersten Sonnenstrahlen.

The monopteros in the park of Linderhof Castle welcoming the first rays of sunlight.

73

Erster Schnee am Geroldsee. Links über dem Schilf die Berge der Soierngruppe mit der Schöttelkarspitze. Nach rechts schließt sich die Karwendelgruppe mit Wörner, Tiefkarspitze, Westlicher Karwendelspitze und Linderspitze an.

The first snow on Lake Gerold. On the left, above the reeds, the mountains of the Soiern range, with the peak of Schöttelkar. On the right, the adjacent Karwendel range, with Wörner and the peaks of Tiefkar, Western Karwendel and Linder.

Der Geigenbau hat eine lange Tradition in Mittenwald. Die staatliche Berufsfach- und Fachschule für Geigenbau und Zupfinstrumentenmacher hat hier ihren Sitz.

Mittenwald has a long tradition of violin making. The State Vocational College and Technical College for Violin Makers and the Crafting of Plucked Instruments is located here.

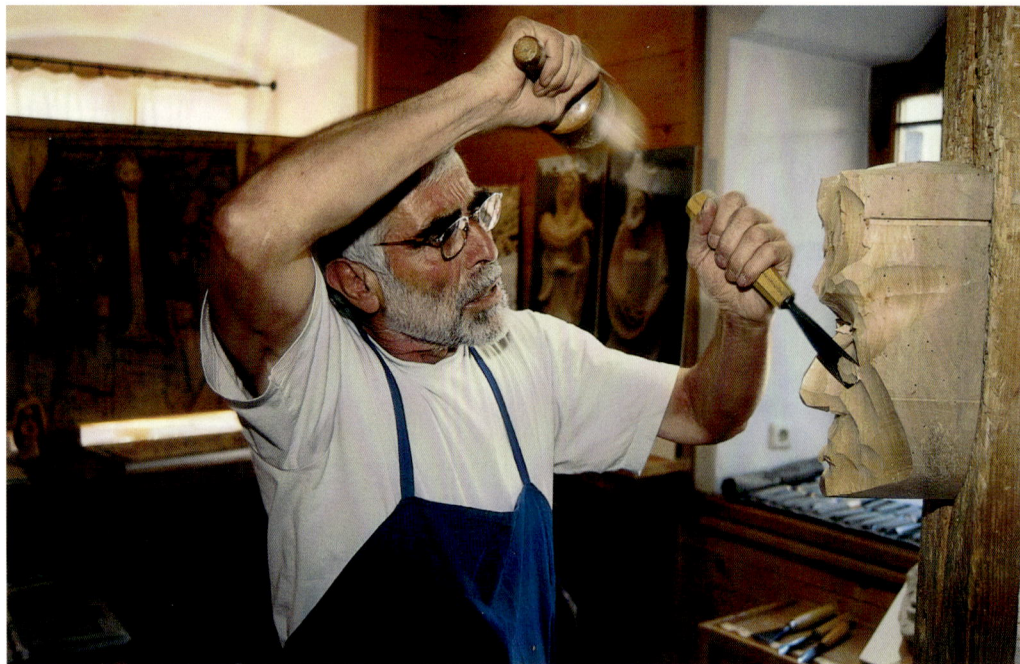

Oberammergau ist auch bekannt durch seine Holzschnitzer. Das Heimatmuseum beherbergt eine reiche Sammlung ausdrucksstarker Kruzifixe und Krippenfiguren.

Oberammergau is also well-known for its wood carvers. The Homeland Museum houses a fine collection of very expressive crucifixes and Nativity figurines.

76

Die mächtige Kuppel der Klosterkirche Ettal mit dem großen Decken-
fresko von Johann Jakob Zeiller stammt aus dem 18. Jahrhundert.
Fast südländisch mutet sie an im Kranz der Ammergauer Berge.

The mighty dome of the monastery church of Ettal, with its
large ceiling fresco by Johann Jakob Zeiller, originates from
the 18th century. It strikes us as having almost a Mediterranean
flair, surrounded by the Ammergau mountains.

Doppeltes Aufleuchten der Karwendelberge im Abendlicht
am Schmalensee bei Mittenwald.

The reflection of the Karwendel mountains, lit up by the
evening sun on Lake Schmalen near Mittenwald.

Einsame Spur auf den Buckelwiesen bei Klais –
da werden Winterträume Wirklichkeit.

A lonely track through the Buckel meadows near Klais –
where dreams of winter come true.

Am Fastnachtssonntag
ziehen die „Maschkerer"
mit ihren prachtvollen
Werdenfelser Masken
durch Partenkirchen
und dabei dürfen auch
die „Untersberger
Mandl" nicht fehlen.

On Carnival Sunday,
fancy dress figures
wearing their
superb Werden-
fels masks parade
through Parten-
kirchen, whereby the
Untersberg Dwarves
are also present.

80

Tief verschneit zeigt sich das Eschenloher Moos im Februar.   *Deep snow on Eschenloh Moor in February.*

Es ist nicht weit von der Millionenmetropole München in das Fünfseenland. Etwas scherzhaft spricht man deshalb auch von der Badewanne Münchens. Hier, zwischen Ammersee und Starnberger See, in der buckligen Moränenlandschaft mit ihren hingeduckten Dörfern, den blumengeschmückten Bauernhäusern und den Zwiebeltürmen der Kirchen, weitet sich die Seele angesichts der Blicke auf Wetterstein und Benediktenwand. Auch wenn Föhntage manchem Kopfschmerzen bescheren, diese Tage an Pilsensee, Wörthsee und Weßlinger See vergißt man nicht so leicht.

„Fürstensee" nannte man den Starnberger See auch, hatten doch an seinen Ufern Fürsten, Schriftsteller und Maler ihre Domizile, verträumt liegend in großen Parks mit teilweise exotischen Bäumen. Weil das halt damals in Mode war. Der Ammersee wurde etwas geringschätzig als „Bauernsee" bezeichnet. Das hat ihm aber viel von seiner Ursprünglichkeit bewahrt. Und mit noch etwas ganz Unvergleichlichem kann dieser Ammersee aufwarten. Hoch über seinem Ostufer liegt das Kloster Andechs auf dem „Heiligen Berg" der Oberbayern. 1455 wurde es gegründet. Frömmigkeit und Bierseligkeit, Wallfahrt und Maßkrüge begegnen sich hier in einer Art, die sich nicht gegenseitig ausschließt.

It's not far from the million-strong metropolis of Munich to the Region of the Five Lakes, which is why people speak rather jokingly of its being the "bath tub" of Munich. Here, between Lake Ammer and Lake Starnberg, in the undulating, morainic landscape with its villages huddling between the hills, farmhouses decorated with flowers and the onion towers of the churches, it raises your spirits to look across to Wetterstein and Benediktenwand. Even if the days when the Föhn wind is blowing can cause some people headaches, the days by Lake Pilsen, Lake Wörth and Lake Weßling will not easily be forgotten.

Lake Starnberg was also called the "prince's lake", probably because princes, writers and painters set up domicile on its banks, lying day-dreaming in large parks with trees some of which were exotic. That was the fashion at the time, quite simply. By contrast, Lake Ammer was referred to rather pejoratively as the "peasant's lake", which enabled it to retain much of its originality. And there's something else quite incomparable that Lake Ammer has to offer. High above its eastern bank is situated Andechs Monastery, founded in 1455, atop the "Holy Mountain" of the Upper Bavarians. Piety and good-natured inebriation, pilgrimages and beer mugs come together here in such a way that isn't mutually exclusive.

Das Fünfseenland

Klosterbier und Zwiebeltürme vor imposanter Bergkulisse

The Region of the Five Lakes – Monastery beer and onion towers against an imposing mountain backdrop

Bei St. Heinrich am Ostufer des Starnberger Sees. Die Sonne ist schon untergegangen, der Abend schenkt uns in der „blauen Stunde" Stille und Besinnung.

Near St. Heinrich, on the east bank of Lake Starnberg. The sun has already set, and the evening rewards us with calm and contemplation for an hour or so.

Üppig und prachtvoll ist der Blumenschmuck an diesem Bauernhaus in Bernried am Starnberger See. Wird da nicht der Wunsch wach, unter diesem Dach zu nächtigen, auf diesem Balkon zu sitzen? An Mariä Himmelfahrt verzaubern zahllose Kerzen die Häuser.

An ornate abundance of flowers decorate this farmhouse in Bernried on Lake Starnberg. Doesn't it make you want to spend the night here and sit on the balcony? On Assumption Day the houses look enchanted, adorned with a multitude of candles.

Abend am Westufer des Ammersees bei Riederau.   *Evening on the west bank of Lake Ammer, near Riederau.*

Maibaum neben Kirchturm, Frömmigkeit neben weltlicher Festes-
freude am Marktplatz in Erling unterhalb des Klosters Andechs.

A May tree beside the church tower, piety juxtaposed
with a secular feast day on the market square in Erling,
beneath Andechs Monastery.

Der Zwiebelturm der Kirche von Münsing durchbricht die vom
Abendlicht gefärbte Bergkette der Ammergauer Berge.

The onion tower of the church in Münsing cuts into the range of the
Ammergau mountains, steeped in the evening light.

Mysteriös bleibt der Tod des Märchenkönigs Ludwig II. im Starnberger See bis heute. Dieses Gedenkkreuz erinnert an jenen 13. Juni 1886.

The death of the fairy tale king Ludwig II in Lake Starnberg remains a mystery to this day. This memorial cross reminds us of that fateful 13 June 1886.

Zum Fünfseenland gehören auch die versteckten Weiher wie hier bei Machtlfing. Große und kleine Wasser ganz nah nebeneinander.

The Region of the Five Lakes also includes hidden ponds, like this one near Machtlfing. Waters large and small adjacent to one another.

Man sollte sich dem Kloster Andechs auf dem „Heiligen Berg" zu Fuß nähern, am besten von Herrsching aus. Das ist respektvoll, gestattet ein Sicheinstimmen und führt dann zu jener Harmonie von Geist und Körper, von Barock und Biergarten.

The best way of reaching Andechs Monastery atop the "Holy Mountain" is on foot from Herrsching. Not only is this more respectful, it also allows you time to contemplate and attain harmony between body and soul, between baroque and beer garden.

Zwischen November und März ruht die Schiffahrt auf den bayerischen Seen. Auch der kleine Dampfer „Münsing" wartet an der Tutzinger Anlegestelle auf die nächste Saison.

Between November and March, shipping on Bavaria's lakes is suspended. The little steamer "Münsing" also awaits the start of the next season at the landing stage in Tutzing.

Stege und alte Boots-
häuser in Dießen am
Ammersee.

Jetties and old boat
houses in Dießen, on
Lake Ammer.

Im Eis gefangen –
Detail eines
Holzsteges am
Starnberger See.

Trapped in the ice
– close-up of a
wooden jetty on
Lake Starnberg.

*Der Föhn rückt Zugspitzmassiv und Kloster Andechs zusammen.
70 Kilometer schrumpfen, die Berge sind zum Greifen nahe.*

*The Föhn wind makes the Zugspitze massif and Andechs
Monastery appear close together. 45 miles are reduced to nothing,
the mountains look as if they're near enough to touch.*

*Die Natur beschenkt uns oft mit unwirklich erscheinenden Farb-
spielen am Himmel, alle paar Minuten wechselnd,
sich spiegelnd im Starnberger See. Fotografiert von der
Ilkahöhe oberhalb von Tutzing.*

*Nature often rewards us with surrealistic-looking iridescence in
the sky, changing every couple of minutes, and reflecting on Lake
Starnberg. Photographed from Ilka Heights, above Tutzing.*

Zu Füßen der Ammergauer und Tannheimer Berge erstreckt sich das Ostallgäu mit einer geradezu heiteren Landschaft, sanft wellig geformt, mit versteckten Seen und Weihern, wie etwa der Bannwaldsee, der Schapfensee oder der Hergartsrieder Weiher. Der große Forggensee ist erst in den 1950er Jahren dazugekommen, als man den Lech aufgestaut hat.

Eine der bekanntesten Rokokokirchen Deutschlands, die Wieskirche, mit ihrer Wallfahrt „Zum gegeißelten Heiland" ist hier zu finden, und das barocke St. Coloman bei Schwangau zierte schon unzählige Kalender. Ja, es ist dieses Zusammenklingen von Hügeln, den nicht auftrumpfenden Bergen als Kulisse für diese Kirchen, welche einen harmonischen Eindruck hinterlassen.

Neben diesen Kirchen sind es natürlich die Königsschlösser, die Touristen aus aller Welt in diese Landschaft ziehen. Was wäre ein Europatrip für viele Amerikaner und Japaner ohne Hohenschwangau und vor allem Neuschwanstein, diesem romantischen Traumschloß des Märchenkönigs auf steilem Fels über der Pöllatschlucht? Hier wurde er festgenommen vor seinem Tod im Starnberger See, um den sich auch heute noch viele Rätsel ranken. „Königswinkel", wohl zu Recht verdient dies Land solch ein Prädikat.

At the foot of the mountains of Ammergau and Tannheim, the region of East Allgäu stretches out with its pleasantly cheerful countryside, gently undulating, with hidden lakes and ponds such as Lake Bannwald, Lake Schapfen or Hergartsrieder Pond. The large Lake Forggen was not added until the 1950s, when a dam was built on the River Lech.

One of the most famous rococo churches in Germany, the Wieskirche, with its pilgrimage called "The Lashing of the Saviour" can be found here, and the baroque church of St. Coloman near Schwangau has already been depicted on numerous calendars. Indeed, it's this unison of hills with mountains that do not brag, as a backdrop for these churches, which leaves you with such an impression of harmony.

Apart from the churches, of course, it's the royal castles that attract tourists from all over the world to this region. What would a trip to Europe be for some of the Americans and Japanese without Hohenschangau Castle and, above all, Neuschwanstein Castle, the romantic, dreamlike castle which the fairy tale king had built on a steep rockface above the Gorge of Pöllat? This is where he was arrested before he drowned in Lake Starnberg, something that still today is steeped in mystery. This region well deserves the name "Königswinkel" (King's Corner).

Der Königswinkel – das Ostallgäu
Märchenschlösser vor traumhafter Kulisse
Königswinkel – East Allgäu – Fairy tale castles in a picturesque landscape

Der herbstliche Morgennebel gibt nur zögernd den Blick auf den Illasbergsee und das Ammergebirge frei.
Autumnal morning mist hesitatingly permits us a view of Lake Illasberg and the Ammer mountains.

Allgäuer Braunvieh inmitten blühender Wiesen.

Brown Allgäu cows amidst blossoming meadows.

Anfang Mai überziehen die Löwenzahnwiesen die Landschaft wie hier bei der Ortschaft Seeg.

At the beginning of May, the landscape is covered with fields of dandelion, like here at the hamlet of Seeg.

St. Coloman bei
Schwangau bietet das
unverfälschte Bild einer
Wallfahrtskirche aus
dem frühen bayerischen
Barock. Alljährlich
findet am 2. Oktober-
sonntag ein Umritt vor
prächtiger Kulisse statt.

St. Coloman's, near
Schwangau, exemplifies
a genuine pilgrimage
church from the early
Bavarian baroque
period. Every year, on
the second Sunday in
October, a parade takes
place against a
magnificent backdrop.

Im Schapfensee bei Kniebis spiegeln sich die markanten Gipfel der Ammergauer, der Säuling und der Hohe Straußberg.

The prominent peaks of Ammergauer, Säuling and Hoher Strauß-berg reflected in Lake Schapfen, near Kniebis.

Am späten Abend kommt nach dem Durchzug einer Schlecht-wetterfront doch noch einmal die Sonne durch und läßt das Schilf am nördlichen Ufer des Forggensees golden aufleuchten.

Late in the evening, after the bad weather has passed, the sun comes out once again, lending a golden hue to the reeds on the north bank of Lake Forggen.

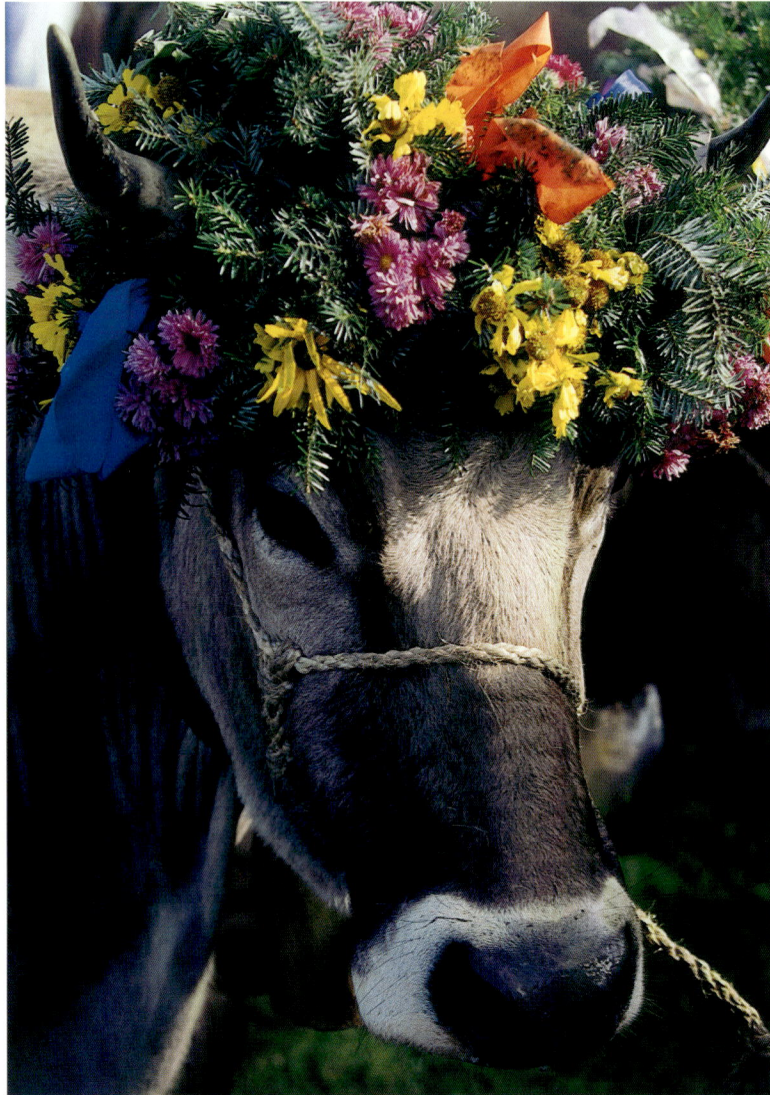

Prächtig geschmückte Kühe und Rösser beim Viehmarkt in Buching. Es wird gehandelt und gefeilscht, bis ein Handschlag das Geschäft besiegelt.

Magnificently decorated cows and horses at the cattle market in Buching. Bargaining and haggling goes on until a deal is concluded by handshake.

Zu Ehren des heiligen Georg, dem Schutzpatron der Rösser, versammeln sich auf dem Auerberg bei Bernbeuren die Reiter, um an der feierlichen Feldmesse teilzunehmen und den Georgischwur zu erneuern.

In honour of St. George, the patron saint of horses, riders gather on Auerberg, near Bernbeuren, to participate in the ceremonious mass held in the field and renew their oath to the saint.

Inneres und Äußeres in harmonischer Vollendung: die Wieskirche
„Zum gegeißelten Heiland" in der Nähe von Steingaden, errichtet
nach den Plänen von Dominikus Zimmermann und mit Fresken
und Stukkaturen von Johann Baptist Zimmermann.

Interior and exterior in harmonious perfection: Wies church,
"The Lashing of the Saviour", near Steingaden, constructed to
plans by Dominikus Zimmermann and with frescoes and
stucco work by Johann Baptist Zimmermann.

*Schloß Hohenschwangau, beleuchtet in der Dämmerung
vor den Gipfeln der Tannheimer Kette.*

*Hohenschwangau Castle lit up in the twilight against
the summits of the Tannheim range.*

Alphornbläser aus dem gesamten Allgäu nehmen jedes Jahr lautstark an der Bergmesse auf dem Breitenberg oberhalb von Pfronten teil.

In strident tones, Alpine horn blowers from all over Allgäu take part in the mountain mass every year up on Breitenberg, above Pfronten.

Der freistehende Auerberg, auch „schwäbischer Rigi" genannt, bietet zu jeder Jahreszeit einen phantastischen Rundumblick aufs Alpenvorland.

Because it stands alone, you have fantastic panoramic views of the Alpine foreland at all times of year from Auerberg, also known as "Swabian Rigi".

Der Alpsee, unterhalb der Märchenschlösser gelegen.

Lake Alp, lying beneath the fairy tale castles.

Über der Stadt Füssen thronen das Hohe Schloß, früher die
Sommerresidenz der Augsburger Fürstbischöfe, und das ehemalige
Benediktinerkloster St. Mang.

Above the town of Füssen, as if enthroned, the High Castle,
once the summer residence of the Augsburg prince bishops,
and the former Benedictine monastery of St. Mang.

Türme, Zinnen und Erker auf Schloß Neuschwanstein –
hier sind die Träume eines Königs zu Stein geworden. Heißt es
deswegen Märchenschloß und Märchenkönig?

Towers, battlements and oriel windows of Neuschwanstein
Castle – this is where the dreams of a king turned to stone. Is that
why we speak of a fairy tale castle and a fairy tale king?

Die angezuckerten Gipfel der Tannheimer Kette steigen hinter dem Bannwaldsee auf. See, Wald und Berge bilden auch hier einen harmonischen Dreiklang.

As if sprinkled with sugar, the summits of the Tannheim Range tower up behind Lake Bannwald. Lake, forest and mountains combine here to form a harmonious triad.

Letztes Aufleuchten spätherbstlicher Bäume vor verschneiten Gipfeln und Bergwäldern. Um diese Zeit ist man oft völlig alleine unterwegs.

For the last time, trees in late autumn glow against snow-covered peaks and mountain forests. It's at times like this that you can be out and about in complete solitude.

113

Oberallgäu, das ist das Land zwischen Oberstdorf, Oberstaufen, Kempten und der Wertach. Da denkt man an grüne Matten, Kirchtürme ducken sich hinter Löwenzahnwiesen und blühende Obstbäume stehen als weiße Tupfer in der Landschaft. Dem Bodensee zu senkt sich die Landschaft, hier reiht sich Apfelbaum an Apfelbaum. In der Ferne glitzert der See, Segelbote kreuzen und am jenseitigen Ufer, im Dunst eines Sommertages, liegen Österreich und die Schweiz. Ganze Radlerkolonnen umrunden den See, schmucke Wirtshäuser laden zur Einkehr und die Abendsonne bringt den See zum Leuchten, manchmal unwirklich schön. Wasserburg und Lindau sind die bayerischen Städte am „alemannischen Meer" im südwestlichsten Zipfel Bayerns.

Früher wurde im Oberallgäu viel Flachs angebaut, man sprach vom „blauen Allgäu", der Flachsblüte wegen. Heute dominiert die Vieh- und Milchwirtschaft. Etwa 100 Tage dauert der Alpsommer und im September ist Viehscheid. Das reich geschmückte Vieh wird von den Hirten ins Tal getrieben und dort geschieden, das heißt, den einzelnen Bauern übergeben. Man ist dankbar, wenn Mensch und Tier vom Unglück verschont wurden.

Upper Allgäu is the area between Oberstdorf, Oberstaufen, Kempten and the River Wertach, where we think of green meadows, church spires peeping out from behind fields of dandelion, and fruit trees in full bloom standing like specks of white in the landscape.

The countryside slopes down towards Lake Constance, with row upon row of apple trees. In the distance you can see the lake glistening, sailing boats crossing and, on the opposite shore and just visible on a hazy summer's day, are Austria and Switzerland. Whole convoys of cyclists ride round the lake, spruce little guesthouses invite the thirsty traveller to enter, and the evening sun lights up the lake sometimes so beautifully that it seems unreal. Wasserburg and Lindau are the Bavarian towns by the "Alemannic Lake" in this south-westernmost tip of Bavaria.

Earlier, a lot of flax was cultivated in Upper Allgäu; hence, it's been nicknamed "Blue Allgäu" because of the flax blossom. Today, the cattle and dairy industries predominate. The Alpine summer lasts about 100 days, and in September the tradition of "Viehscheid" takes place, whereby the richly ornamented cow is driven down into the valley and symbolically passed over to the individual farmers. People are grateful if both man and beast have been spared misfortune.

Vom Oberallgäu zum Bodensee
Glückliche Kühe und blühende Obstgärten

From Upper Allgäu to Lake Constance – Contented cows and blossoming orchards

Inmitten blühender Obstbäume lugt die Kirche des Ortes Unterreitnau über sattgrünen Wiesen hervor.
Amidst blossoming fruit trees, the church in the hamlet of Unterreitnau peeps out above luscious green meadows.

Im bayerisch-württembergischen Grenzgebiet finden sich noch zahllose alte und knorrige Obstbäume. Man denkt schon jetzt an wohlschmeckende Äpfel alter Sorten, vielleicht auch an den guten Most.

In the region along the border between Bavaria and Württemberg there are still countless old, gnarled fruit trees. Now's the time people start thinking about the different, tasty sorts of apples, perhaps also about the good cider to come.

116

Ländliches Idyll unter blühenden Bäumen. Die Kaltblüter-Pferde genießen die letzten Sonnenstrahlen, die Lichtsäume zeichnen und den Atem sichtbar werden lassen.

An idyllic country scene beneath blossoming trees. Heavy horses enjoying the last rays of the sun, edged with light, their breath visible as a result.

*Die einladende Lindauer Seepromenade mit ihrem Wahrzeichen,
dem Mangturm, ehemals der Leuchtturm der Stadt.*

*The lake promenade of Lindau is an inviting prospect with its
landmark, the Mang Tower, once the town's lighthouse.*

*Wie eine kleine Insel im großen Bodensee erscheint die
Lindauer Altstadt. Vom Aussichtsberg Pfänder in Vorarlberg hat
man diesen großartigen Blick.*

*The old town centre of Lindau looks like a little island compared
with great Lake Constance. This gorgeous view
is from the Pfänder mountaintop outlook point in Vorarlberg.*

118

Argwöhnisch beäugen die vierbeinigen Rindviecher das zweibeinige Wesen mit dem Dreibein. Am Stoffelberg oberhalb des Niedersonthofener Sees.

Four-legged cattle suspiciously eyeing a two-legged creature with a tripod. On Stoffelberg, above Lake Niedersonthofen.

120

Impressionen von der Viehscheid im Gunzesrieder Tal. Für die Hirten ist jetzt ein arbeitsreiches Jahr zu Ende.

Impressions of the tradition of passing cattle over in Gunzesrieder valley. For the farmers, a hard year's work has come to an end.

Verträumt noch, die Dämmerung ist erst vor kurzem gewichen, beleuchten die ersten Sonnenstrahlen die Pfarrkirche St. Georg in Wasserburg.

Still dreamlike, the day has only just dawned and the first rays of the sun light up the parish church of St. George in Wasserburg.

Morgen am Niedersonthofener See. Landschaft und Wasser scheinen zu glühen, eine Stimmung, die nur wenige Minuten andauert.

Morning on Lake Niedersonthofen. Both landscape and water look as if they're alight, a mood that lasts but a few minutes.

124

Nur der Gesang der Vögel war an diesem Morgen am Alpsee vor den Toren Immenstadts zu hören.

Only the song of the birds could be heard this morning by Lake Alp, just outside the town gates of Immenstadt.

Der Winter ist eingekehrt im Allgäu. In den Holzhütten lagert das Heu für die Fütterung der Tiere im Stall. Im Hintergrund das 2224 m hohe Nebelhorn.

Winter has come to Allgäu. In the wooden huts, the hay for feeding the animals in the stables and sheds has been stored. In the background Nebelhorn, 7,295 ft high.

Oberstdorf ist ein gut besuchter Kneipp- und heilklimatischer Kurort. Seine Umgebung lädt ein zu Wanderungen und Bergtouren, die Breitachklamm will erkundet werden und bei der Vierschanzentournee herrscht Hochbetrieb im südlichsten Ort Bayerns.

With its healthy climate and hydrotherapy, Oberstdorf is a very popular health resort. The surrounding countryside invites enthusiasts to take hikes and mountain tours, Breitachklamm waits to be discovered, and when the Four Hills Tournament is taking place there's a bustle of activity in this southernmost town in Bavaria.

127

Bernd Römmelt (re.), geboren 1968 in München. Nach dem Studium der Betriebswirtschaftslehre, schloß er ein Studium der Völkerkunde an. Schon während der Studienzeit 13 Fotoreisen nach Alaska und Kanada. Seit 2000 arbeitet er als freiberuflicher Fotograf für in- und ausländische Agenturen und veröffentlicht regelmäßig in Zeitschriften und Büchern. Auszeichnungen im wichtigsten Naturfotowettbewerb „Wildlife Photographer of the Year" der BBC. Neben seiner Heimat Oberbayern stellen die nordischen Länder Alaska, Skandinavien und Grönland die wichtigsten Arbeitsgebiete dar.

Bernd Römmelt (right), born in Munich in 1968. Studied business administration, then ethnology. During his studies, 13 photographic trips to Alaska and Canada. Since 2000 he has worked as a freelance photographer for agencies in and outside Germany, and publishes regularly in magazines and books. Awards in the most prestigious nature photographic competition, the BBC's "Wildlife Photographer of the Year". Apart from his native region of Upper Bavaria, the Nordic countries of Alaska, Scandinavia and Greenland are his most important fields of work.

Bildnachweis:
Bernd Römmelt: S. 2, S. 5, S. 9, S. 10, S. 11, S. 12, S. 13, S. 14/15, S. 16, S. 17, S. 18/19, S. 20, S. 21, S. 23, S. 24, S. 25, S. 26, S. 27, S. 28, S. 29, S. 30, S. 31, S. 32, S. 33, S. 34/35, S. 37, S. 38, S. 39, S. 40, S. 41, S. 42, S. 43, S. 44/45, S. 46, S. 47, S. 48, S. 49, S. 52 oben rechts, unten rechts, S. 54, S. 55, S. 56 oben, S. 58, S. 68, S. 69, S. 70, S. 71, S. 72, S. 76, S. 77, S. 78, S. 79, S. 80, S. 81, S. 84, S. 87, S. 88, S. 92, S. 94, S. 95, Umschlagrückseite

Michael Lechner: Titel, S. 1, S. 51, S. 52 oben links, unten links, S. 53, S. 56 unten, S. 57, S. 59, S. 60, S. 61, S. 62, S. 63, S. 64/65, S. 67, S. 73, S. 74/75, S. 83, S. 85, S. 86, S. 89, S. 90/91, S. 93, S. 97, S. 98, S. 99, S. 100/101, S. 102, S. 103, S. 104, S. 105, S. 106, S. 107, S. 108, S. 109, S. 110, S. 111, S. 112, S. 113, S. 115, S. 116, S. 117, S. 118, S. 119, S. 120, S. 121, S. 122/123, S. 124, S. 125, S. 126, S. 127, S. 128

Michael Lechner (li.), geboren 1969 in München. Nach dem Abitur Studium der Ethnologie, Amerikanistik und Sozialpsychologie. Seit 1989 umfangreiche Fotoreisen nach Mittel- und Südamerika, Nordamerika, Indonesien und Australien. Ganz ernsthaft betreibt er die Fotografie seit 1998. Neben seiner Heimat Oberbayern und dem Allgäu hat es ihm vor allem Slowenien angetan. Aber auch der Osten Kanadas zieht ihn immer wieder an.

Michael Lechner (left), born in Munich in 1969. Read ethnology, American studies and social psychology. Since 1989 he has undertaken extensive photographic trips to Central and South America, North America, Indonesia and Australia. He has only seriously indulged in photography since 1998. In addition to his native region of Upper Bavaria and Allgäu, he is particularly fond of Slovenia and the many attractions of the east of Canada.

Zur Fotografie
Alle Bilder im Buch sind mit analogen Kleinbildkameras entstanden. Es kamen dabei Brennweiten von 18 bis 600 mm zum Einsatz. Die Panoramabilder wurden mit der Hasselblad X Pan fotografiert. Als Filmmaterial wurden der Fuji Velvia und Kodak Elite Extra Color verwendet. Die Bilder wurden nicht digital verändert.

About the photography
All the photographs in this book were taken with analogue 35 mm cameras, using focal lengths from 18 to 600 mm. The panoramas were photographed with a Hasselblad X Pan; films in use were Fuji Velvia and Kodak Elite Extra Color. The photographs have not been digitally enhanced.

In der „Naturreihe" des Buch & Kunstverlags Oberpfalz sind noch folgende Titel erschienen:
„Wälder – Weite Wildnis – Nationalpark Bayerischer Wald"
„Naturerlebnis Franken – Streifzüge durch eine Seelenlandschaft"
„Die Wildkatze – Zurück auf leisen Pfoten"
„Wolfspuren in Bayern – Kulturgeschichte eines sagenhaften Tieres"
„Sehnsucht Wildnis – Gespür für Leben neu entdecken"
Das gesamte Verlagsprogramm auch im Internet unter: www.buch-und-kunstverlag.de

Visit www.buch-und-kunstverlag.de to see other publications by Buch & Kunstverlag Oberpfalz in the "Nature Series".